From Desperation to Destiny

From Desperation to Destiny

Printed in the United States of America
©2007 by Rhonda Skinner Sullivan
Publisher: We Family Ministries
       P.O. Box 40644
       Jacksonville, FL 32203

Library of Congress Cataloging pending
ISBN: 0-9788545-2-7

TABLE OF CONTENTS

FOREWORD

"But God chose the foolish things of the world to shame the wise; God chose the weak things of the world to shame the strong."
(1 Corinthians 1:27)

Who is more weak than a woman who had been barred from human contact, including public worship for 12 years? Who is more foolish than a woman who spends all of her money looking for a cure to an unknown disease, all while she continues to get worse? How foolish is it to risk your life to claim healing from a man you don't even know? God used the woman with the issue of blood to do just that. She did all of these things, yet because of her humility God was able to use her in a mighty way. For thousands of years her story has been used to teach Christians about faith. But her life stands for so much more. It provides a life-altering example of grace, mercy, redemption, and hope. Her life teaches us lessons about perseverance, faith, strength, courage, obedience, and healing. She teaches us about life.

Although many things are unknown about her, she makes the portrait of a life that pleases God unmistakable. The Bible never tells us if she was a Christian yet she teaches us many of the basic biblical principles necessary for life. It is unknown if she was married, single, or divorced yet she provides an in-depth lesson about the rewards of submission, humility, and love. Her age was never stated but she so clearly shows the true source of wisdom. It does not come with age, as many of us have been taught; it comes from the Lord. The word of God provides little evidence about what kind of disease she had, her symptoms, nor their effect on her yet she inspires us to overcome sickness through her awesome story of healing and restoration. Her life provides one of the greatest examples of how to claim the promises of God through perseverance and obedience. The life of the woman with the issue of blood provides everything you need to know to gain success in life and victory over whatever binds you.

THEY CALL HER "BLESSED"

Blessed is he who transgressions are forgiven,
whose sins are covered.
(Psalms 32:1)

Who is this woman with an issue of blood?
Details of her life of the woman with an issue of blood are provided in Matthew 9,
Mark 5, and Luke 8. Even though her story
is told in three different books of the Bible,
so little is known about her. She has no
name, no nationality, no religious affiliation,
and no place where she belongs. During the
research phase of this book, I hoped to give
her an identity so that you, the reader would
have someone to relate to. I searched the
scriptures, the concordance, and numerous
historical books. There was little to be discovered. I searched unsuccessfully through
genealogical data hoping to give her a name
or a face. In my determination to find answers, I took my search to the Lord. I
asked, "Who is she?" His answer was simple
and direct, **"SHE IS YOU"**. What an awesome revelation. The woman with the issue
of blood is all of us. She is you and me. She
is anyone who has ever faced a trial. She is
that person who needs healing and the one
who has healed and been restored. She is

your mother, your father, your sisters and brothers, your friends. Mark 5:24-34 allows us to take the most in-depth glimpse into her life. It will be used as a template for showing you how to make the promises of God a reality for your life. All scripture is taken from the New International Version translation unless otherwise noted. Bolding provides author emphasis to statements of interest. Many of which will be elaborated on in later text.

24 *So Jesus went with him. A large crowd followed and* **pressed around him.**

25 *And a woman was there who had been* **subject to bleeding for twelve years.**

26 *She had* **suffered a great deal** *under the* **care of many doctors** *and had* **spent all** **she had,** *yet instead of getting better she* **grew worse.**

27 *When* **she heard about Jesus,** *she came up behind him in the crowd and touched his cloak,*

28 *because* **she thought,** *"If I just touch his clothes, I will be healed."*

29 **Immediately** *her bleeding stopped and she felt in her body that* **she was freed** *from her suffering.*

30 *At once* **Jesus realized that power had gone out from him.** *He turned around in the crowd and asked, "Who touched my clothes?"*

31 *"You see the* **people crowding against you,"** *his disciples answered, "and yet you can ask, 'Who touched me?' "*

32 *But Jesus kept* **looking** *around to see who had done it.*

33 *Then the woman, knowing what had happened to her, came and* **fell at his feet and, trembling with fear,** *told him the whole truth.*

34 *He said to her, "* **Daughter, your faith has healed you.** *Go in* **peace** *and* **be freed** *from your suffering."*

Despite all of the unknowns about the woman with the issue of blood, one thing is for sure. She was blessed! She endured twelve years of an incurable illness and lived. She was made rich in the midst of her poverty and received healing from a man she did not know. She was freed from her suffering in the presence of her transgressors. Yet, none of these are the sole reason for her being blessed. Psalm 32:1 says that those whose transgressions are forgiven and sins are covered are blessed. For this reason, I have named the woman with the issue of blood, **"Blessed"**. She was blessed because God's word says she was and God cannot lie! (Titus 1:2)

IN HIS PRESENCE

*24 So Jesus went with him. A large crowd fol-
lowed and pressed around him.*

Mark 5:21-23 describes the plight of
Jairus, a ruler of the synagogue. Jairus ap-
proaches Jesus seeking healing for his
daughter who was dying. As Jesus followed
Jairus to the place where his daughter was, a
crowd followed. In the crowd was a woman
who had been bleeding for twelve years.
Even in the midst of the task at hand, Jesus
stops to heal the woman of her infirmity.
Through this passage of scripture, the
woman with the issue of blood imparts the
importance of getting in the presence of
God.
   According to the law, Blessed was deemed
untouchable by her illness. But she did not
let this distort her Truth. She recognized
the power of God as an available source for
her. In his presence she found the boldness
and strength necessary to claim what she
knew was hers and make the promises of
God a reality for her life. She understood
the importance of developing intimacy as a
point of contact and that doing so allowed
her to claim his promises. In his presence
she found love for the unloved, healing for

hurt, and freedom for the oppressed. There, she, the sinner found redemption and the obedient found reward.

God's word promises that with faith and obedience, you can have the desires of your heart and his word is true. He is faithful to fulfill 'all' of his promises. The woman with the issue of blood brings to life the healing, restoration, love, joy, hope, and peace that can be found in Jesus' presence. She shows us the magnitude of God's love, even in our sins. Her life conveys how all of our needs are priority to God and that knowing this offers hope. This hope brings life.

Blessed's life provides a pathway to understanding God's requirements for obtaining his promises. Her life teaches us how to live a life that is pleasing to God. God will reward those who diligently seek him. (Hebrews 11:6) God does not expect you to get free from sin before you come to Him. He desires and requires your intimacy with him. If you are willing to change, he is able to transform you for his glory

All of our needs are equally important to God. God did not tell the woman with the issue of blood that she had to wait. He did not clarify the importance of a dying child over her needs. He met her needs completely, right then and there. He will do the same for you. No matter what type of life you have been living, how long you've been living it, nor how severe its consequences; God holds you in high esteem. You are equally entitled to his grace and mercy. All he requires it that you invite him in.

God is never too busy to answer your cries for help. Here you have a man whose daughter is dying and he recognizes that Jesus is the only one who can heal her. For many of us, a dying child would prove an emergency or top priority. As it was for Jesus. Yet, he took time to meet the needs of his other child, the woman with the issue of blood, as well. In his eyes, her needs were just as important as Jairus'. He not only healed her, he took time to reassure her of his love for her and to set her totally free her from her suffering. The Word says he made her whole. God is never too busy to wrap his arms around you and shower you with his love. He hears your prayers, he knows your needs, and longs to answer your cries for help.

The large crowd that surrounded Jesus did so because they were seeking some measure of shelter from their storms of life. Maybe they heard of Jesus' power, his teachings, his forgiveness and compassion, or his mighty works. Maybe, they simply recognized the power in his presence. As he walked through that crowd, Jesus did not seek out the rich, the sinless, nor the self-righteous to perform his miracles. As a matter of fact, the Bible reveals Jesus' heart for the sinful, the broken-hearted, and the poor. Matthew 9:12 says that only the sick need a doctor. When Jairus and the woman with the issue approached him, he did not hesitate to meet their needs. He knew their past, their sins, and their pain, yet when they humbly asked he unconditionally answered.

You must do the same. Waiting to be sin-free before coming to God is like standing out in the rain waiting to dry off. It just won't happen. Free your will and allow him to free you from the bondage that controls you. Draw near to him and he will draw near to you. This relationship is your point of contact. It gives you access to his power. Reach out to him and he will meet you right where you are. Cast your cares on him. He can and will handle your situations. When you feel isolated, unloved, or untouchable, remember that your heavenly Father is always there waiting to bless you with the desires of your heart.

In his presence he will heal you from the hurts of life and transform you beyond anything you could ever hope for. In Jesus, there is boldness for meek, courage for the fearful, forgiveness for the sinner, restoration for the broken, and healing for all kinds of sickness.

These principles are not limited to the woman with the issue of blood. These are guidelines for your life as well. Deuteronomy 12:7 states that in the presence of the Lord, you shall eat and rejoice in everything you put your hand to. Are you hungry for some healing? Tired of failure after failure? Need a little joy in your life? In his presence there is shelter for your storm and shade for your heat. In times of your deepest pain, the Lord's presence provides comfort. It provides hope. In his presence there is power, strength, boldness, and freedom. He embraced your pain, humiliation, and shame on the cross. Therefore, it has no place in your life, today. Allow Jesus to heal you, restore you, and make you whole. The power in his presence will help you to claim the desires of your heart and propel you into a place of abundant blessing.

TOUCHING THE UNTOUCHEABLE

Now that you know that getting in the presence of God offers presence, you must know learn how to touch the untouchable. It is as simple as asking in prayer. First I must remove the myths regarding prayer as many of them hindered the effectiveness of my prayers for many years. The removal of misconceptions regarding prayer is as simple as basing your prayer life on one scripture. In John 14:6 Jesus says, "I am the way and the truth and the life. No one comes to the Father except through me." This scripture reminds us that the our prayers must be carried to God through Jesus Christ. We must acknowledge that he is and believe in faith that he will intercede on our behalf. Knowing this requires that you develop a life of intimacy with Jesus Christ through your obedience to God's word. The prayers of the righteous are effective. (James 5:16)

TRIAL AT THE BLOOD FOUNTAIN

*25 And a woman was there who had been **subject to bleeding for twelve years**.*

The woman with the issue of blood was "subject to bleeding for twelve years". The word "subject" implies that her bleeding impacted her life in a substantial way; it controlled her. The Living Word translation refers to her infirmity as a "fountain of blood". To understand the magnitude to which she was blessed, you must understand her trial. Jewish law stated that sickness was the result of sin and any flow of bodily fluid would result in ceremonial defilement. According to Jewish law, she was not only forbidden from contact with other people but she was barred from worship in the synagogue. These restrictions are described in Leviticus 15:25-30a.

When a woman has a discharge of blood for many days at a time other than her monthly period or has a discharge that continues beyond her period, she will be unclean as long as she has the discharge, just as in the days of her period. Any bed she lies on while her discharge continues will be unclean, as is her bed during her monthly period, and anything she sits on will be unclean, as during her period. Whoever touches them will be

unclean; he must was his clothes and bath with water, and he
will be unclean till evening. When she is cleansed from her
discharge, she must count off seen days, and after that she will
be ceremonially clean. On the eighth day she must take two
doves or two young pigeons and bring them to the priest at the
entrance to the Tent of Meeting. The priest is to sacrifice one
for a sin offering and the other for a burnt offering.

Although Jewish law stated that sickness was the result of sin, the Bible does not specifically indicate any sin in Blessed's life. This leads me to believe that her bleeding was not the result of sin but like my abuse, God's trial for propelling her into her purpose. God will allow circumstances to enter your life that demand dependence on him. In the cases of repeated disobedience, God may allow circumstances to overcome you to reduce you to desperation. The Lord knows that in your desperation, you will reach out to him and the woman with the issue of blood did just that. God, through her repeat failed attempts at finding healing, reduced her to desperation. Her trial forced her to reach out to Jesus, knowing that only he could heal her. Through her obedience, she found healing, restoration, and discovered her destiny. Her trial like mine was the catalyst for a testimony for God's glory. It teaches us how to remain focused on the purposes of God even in our trials. Her example portrays the roles of faith, obedience, and humility in our achievement of success. Fulfillment of her destiny provides an undisputed template for your life.

Even in the age of modern medicine, a chronic bleeding disorder would most likely result in a premature death but for Blessed this was not the case. Even though everything in the natural said that she should have been broken, depressed, physically inapt, or dead, she was not. But why wasn't she? There are many reasons. Death was not God's will for her life. She was pre-destined for greatness and God provided supernatural protection over her life so that she would fulfill that purpose. The fulfillment of that plan has provided an amazing example of faith, perseverance, and redemption for thousands of years.

The woman with the issue of blood provides insight into how trials affect our lives and the rewards of perseverance. She faced many storms during her trial. As if the act of bleeding for 12 years was not physically, emotionally, or spiritually devastating enough, the woman with the issue of blood also isolation, disappointment, and failure. She probably experienced many of the same emotions we feel when we face adversity; isolation, loneliness, unworthiness, depression, frustration, or anger. Under these circumstances many of us would become weary; maybe to even give up. But this was not the case with the woman with the issue of blood. She persevered in faith and when the appropriate time came, she was in the right place prepared to receive her blessing and fulfill her purpose.

Blessed's trial is not just a Bible fairy tale. It is an experience that is very real today. It is my story as well. I was married to a violently-abusive spouse for five years. As the abuse worsened, my desire to find solace grew. I, like Blessed, tried all of the ways of the world without success. As failure, disappointment, and pain overcame me, I was reduced to a place where I knew that only God could provide what I was searching for. I reached out to him and my life, like Blessed's was forever changed. The magnitude of my blessing could only be found in the presence of the Lord. I endured beating after beating over the span of five years but when each blow should have made me weaker, through Jesus Christ I grew stronger. As the man who was supposed to love me tried to demean and degrade me, I grew wiser; seeing my self as God sees me. As he tried to steal my life, I began to live in the fullness of God. When each hurtful word should have made me retreat, I ran to the altar. At the altar I not only found protection from my abuser but I discovered my purpose as well.

Even the sparrow finds a home and the swallow a nest near the Lord. Surely there is a place for you at his altar. It is at this altar that the desires of your heart lie. Seek the presence of the great Physician, Jesus Christ. Bring your suffering and sin to him in faith. He has been in the healing business for thousands of years and has a hundred percent success rate. At his altar, there is healing, peace, love, and freedom. When Jesus bore our sins on the cross, he bore our sicknesses and our trials, as well. Blessed's life is a testimony to this. God watches over his word to perform it. He will do what his word says he will do.

In 2 Corinthians, Paul speaks of the trials, hardships, and distresses of believers. He stresses that serving God comes with a price. That price is paid as you endure trials and tribulation with Godly perseverance. Your reward is that as you go through, you will become stronger, wiser, and more equip to bring others to Christ. Paul goes on to say that even when we feel like we have nothing, we have everything. You will be made rich in Jesus. The reward for your perseverance is prosperity and that prosperity comes in the fulfillment of your destiny. God will preserve you for his purpose. He will show you his power so that you will proclaim his name throughout all the earth.

Life will bring you many trials. James 1:2-3 promises this but don't give up. Do not let the trials of life distort who you know you are in Christ. There is a purpose for your trial. It will foster faith and develop perseverance. Your trials will prepare you to occupy your ordained place of purpose in his kingdom. Stand in faith and wait on the Lord. He is always with you and will order your steps for your ultimate good. Trust that his word is true. As trials come, remember the examples set before you. God does not want you to struggle with and stress over the trials of life. He wants you to bring them to him. He will give you the strength to triumph over your circumstances. He will shield you with supernatural protection that will carry you. Remember that no matter what your plans are, the Lord's plan will prevail. You are predestined for a purpose. Fulfilling that purpose, means that you will face adversity but do not be unsettled during your trials. Trials come as a part of his plan to perfect you and they come with a promise. That promise, as detailed in Deuteronomy 7:29, is that God will bring you out of your trials. Face each trial with perseverance and determination knowing that God will preserve you for his purpose.

THE WAY, THE TRUTH, THE LIFE

26 She had suffered a great deal under the care of many doctors and had spent all she had, yet instead of getting better she grew worse.

A mirage is a phenomenon where you think you see water. They are most common in deserts. As Blessed endured twelve years in the desert of her infirmity. For those twelve years without Jesus, her healing and restoration was a mirage. This mirage distracted her away from the source of her healing, Jesus Christ. Throughout her trial, Blessed learns the penalty for the hindrance of distraction. She put her hope in the things of the world; doctors and worldly cures. She spent twelve years looking for worldly answers to a spiritual problem. In response, she faced twelve years of disappointment, failure, and worsening circumstances and it wasn't until she realized where her healing laid that she was able to be healed.

Many of us are not much different. We live in sin searching for the facade of love, healing, prosperity, peace, and happiness. We spend years searching in all the wrong places. Many of us heard about Jesus long before we answered his call. Some of us totally ignored what we heard. Others chose to accept small portions of the message, usually the easy parts. Few of us choose to act on all of his requirements for our life. Like Blessed, we often suffer one defeat after another as we waste precious time searching in all the wrong places for the peace and fulfillment that only God could give. No sickness can be cured by man in the absence of God.

Blessed's sickness is symbolic of sin and how sin will hinder your progress in life. Her infirmity served as a distraction for twelve years. It sent her looking in all the wrong places for her healing. Her illness told her that she was undeserving of the love of others and of God's love. It kept her from coming to know the Lord intimately. Sin will do the same thing in your life. It will prevent you from seeing yourself and your circumstances the way God sees them. He sees you whole and fulfilled and your situations resolved but sin distorts this Truth. Sin can keep you from drawing close to God by making you feel unworthy. It prevents you from worshipping God in the fullness of your calling.

Blessed's poverty was a distraction as well. It was not just financial but more importantly, spiritual. She spent all of her money seeking medical care. The scriptures say that she had "heard of Jesus". This tells us that she did not have a personal relationship with God. Additionally, her illness made her unable to partake of public worship. She lacked the knowledge necessary to live the abundant life that God's word promises. It was in this abundant life that her healing and restoration rested. Her ignorance to the greatness of God hindered her and left an opening for Satan to have power in her life. Think about a life without Jesus. How much more destitute was she because of this than all the money she spent on doctors?

Blessed's life demonstrates how even the poor in spirit can overcome trials of life. Once she gained knowledge of Jesus Christ everything else became available to her. Her knowledge propelled her into ordained place of righteousness. Without a relationship with Jesus, you will not have success over the powers of darkness nor in life. If Satan gains an opportunity to bring sickness, pain, suffering, and death into your life, he will. To overcome his attempts and gain spiritual prosperity, you must accept Jesus into your heart and allow him to control every part of your being. As you do he reveals his love, compassion, and faithfulness to your. Jesus frees you from the bondage that controls you and elevates you into a place of righteousness that places you above your circumstances. Satan and his attempts will have no power in your life.

Be Vigilant. Even Jesus faced distraction in his attempts to fulfill God's plan for his life. His birth, death, the resurrection, and every event in Jesus' life was predestined. Yet Satan was never far from him, always there waiting to hinder God's plan. As Jesus walked through that crowd, even the crowd became a distraction. The crowd seeked to draw his attention from Blessed who was predestined to get her healing at that particular point in time. Even the disciples attempted to distract God by down-playing his awareness of the power that had left his body. But Jesus kept his eye on his destiny. He never wavered from the plans and purpose of God for his life. He never sinned. He was in the crowd just as God planned. Blessed and Jairus were right where they needed to be and all things worked for their ultimate good just as God's word promises. And those he predestined, he also called; those he called, he also justified; those he justified, he also glorified. (Romans 8:30)

In the midst of your trials, you will face distractions as well. Recognize these as works of the devil and stand faithfully on the promises of God to help you overcome.

They are Satan's attempts at hindering you work in the kingdom of God. Bind the spirits of evil that seek to deter you and loose victory in your life.

BY YOUR SPIRIT, LORD

*27 When **she heard about Jesus**, she came up behind him in the crowd and touched his cloak,*

He sent his word and healed them; he rescued them from the grave. (Psalm 107:20). The woman with an issue of blood had only heard of Jesus. The scripture does not say specifically what she heard but it must have been powerful enough to give her hope. Maybe she heard how Jesus had healed the lame, the blind, the crippled, the mute, the demon-possessed, epileptics, and paralytics. Maybe she heard of his compassion toward the sick and the poor. Maybe she heard how many people had been laid at his feet and receive their healing. Whatever she heard, it was enough to encourage her to claim what was hers. She acted in obedience in faith and victory was hers.

So, why didn't Blessed fear harm from the others in the crowd? The woman with the issue of blood was willing to reach out to Jesus despite the risk of harm or death because she recognized that he offered her something that was greater than anything the world could do to her. Greater is He that is in you than he that is in the world. (1

John 4:4) With God through Jesus, all things are possible. In her weakness she found strength. In her discouragement, she found perseverance. In her trial, she found power. Not her own power but the power of God, through Jesus Christ transformed her lowly body and made it like his glorious image.

Ecclesiastes 3:1 says that there is a time for everything. Being in the right place at the right time is essential for receiving all that God has for you. Obedience is the key. Blessed's obedience commanded the presence of God where her healing and restoration was laid up for her. She prepared her mind and body for action. She remained self-controlled and set her hope fully on grace. Jesus gave her the hope she needed to walk, speak, and act in faith. She recognized the promise of healing as a reality and stepped into her destiny. She refused to allow the distractions of fear, poverty, or sickness to hinder her.

Psalm 128:2 says that you will eat the fruit of your labor. Timing and preparation is important to the success of every great event in your life. God never allowed his people to go into a trial without first preparing them for the task at hand. He will do the same for you. Be attentive to God's direction for your life. Do not sit idle waiting for God to do all of the work. Act on what he has called you to do. Allow the Holy Spirit to guide you. Seek out the desires of your heart in faith and they will be yours. Through your obedience, God will deliver you out of your circumstances, problems, and troubles; no matter how severe, how prolonged, or how painful. God's strength and wisdom gives you the faith to accomplish the impossible. Jesus is still in the healing business. He still helps the blind to see, the mute to speak, and the deaf to hear. He still raises the dead. So, no matter what you need, believe that it is yours and it is.

Through her intimate touch of Jesus and the power that enables him to bring everything under his control she claims her healing. Like every good father, Jesus knows the cries his children. He recognized Blessed's cry for help and perceived her need without her having to say a word. Her fingers spoke of her desire for healing and restoration. As Blessed reached out to Jesus, her actions revealed her free will. It allowed the power of Jesus to flow in her life. There is no connection to his power without it. Her touch told Jesus that she welcomed his power to heal her and to transform her.

He will do the same for you. God knows your voice and he hears your cries. He instinctually recognizes your touch as you reach out to him. He knows your needs. It is this intimacy not your acts that bring God's blessings to you. Free your will. Without a willing and obedient heart that acts in faith, God can not release his power to work on your behalf. He will not go against your will. Draw near to God, he will cleanse you from the guilt that hinders you. In the presence of God insecurity and failure cannot exist. When you feel isolated, unloved, or untouchable, remember that through is sacrifice, you are entitled to an abundant life.

Claiming what is yours requires that you seek him. He will be found. (1 Chronicles 28:9) Grabbing his glory demands that you never turn your focus away from him. Reach out like "Blessed" and claim what is yours. Honor God with wholehearted devotion and a willing mind. Don't settle for anything less than wholeness. He is never far from you and because he lives in you, nothing less than righteousness and wholeness can. If you reach out to him, he will reach down from on high and take hold of your needs and circumstances. He will draw you out of the deep waters that seek to overcome you. God will speak into your heart exactly what you need to hear to prevail. He will reclaim you from whatever binds you. Your pain and suffering is no match for his love. God's love will help you to recognize that anything that hinders your work in the kingdom of God will be removed. He will equip you to progress in the things of God, to fulfill your ordained purpose, and to praise his name on high. Your glory will be his and his yours.

THE ORIGIN OF FAITH

28 *because* **she thought,** *"If I just touch his clothes, I will be healed."*

In biblical times, the hem of a garment often incorporated a fringe or a border. This was a command of the law. The presence of fringe or borders was most likely related to a regulation enacted upon the Israelites in Numbers 15:38-39. It states, *"Speak to the Israelites and say to them: 'Throughout the generations to come you are to make tassels on the corners of your garments, with a blue cord on each tassel. You will have these tassels to look at and so you will remember all the commands of the LORD, that you may obey them and not prostitute yourselves by going after the lusts of your own hearts and eyes.* This command was to encourage the Israelites to remember the commands of the Lord and to encourage obedience. Touching the hem of symbolized loyalty, faith, and a covenant between God and the people.

Drawing near to God with a sincere heart in full assurance of faith allows you to touch the hem of Jesus garment. By doing this your heart will be sprinkled and you will be cleansed from a guilty conscience. Your body will be washed with pure water. Blessed recognized the difference between the world and the spirit. She was willing to be as the word of God mandates, different from the world. Blessed was willing to break social taboos to claim her blessing. She fixed her mind on Jesus and when she did, what the world said about her did not matter. Blessed looked past the lies of the world to the promises of God and became unstoppable. She took her circumstances to Jesus in faith and he provided the answers. She found God's promises applicable to her life despite the world telling her that she was not worthy of healing. She acknowledged his power to change her situation.

Touching the hem of Jesus allows you to claiming what God has for you but this requires that you renew your mind. Faith forms as you see yourself through God's eyes. As you envision yourself blameless, whole, and righteous you are able to see his promises for your life as a reality. Recognize that God desires your intimacy with him. He desires to have a relationship with you. It frees your will for God to move on your behalf and gives him control over your life so that you can be used for his purposes. Jesus allowed Blessed to access his power, even in her sickness and he will do the same for you. He did not ask her to go and get clean before coming to him. As a matter of fact, he made no demands on her at all. He healed her instantly and completely. He will do the same for your. He is approachable in every circumstance. As you reach out to him, one hundred percent of the time he is waiting and willing to heal you from whatever binds you.

God counts you worthy of his calling. You are not what the world says you are but what God says you are. You are righteous through Christ Jesus and a joint heir to his kingdom. In the kingdom of God, there is no sickness. Every good purpose of yours will be fulfilled by his power but every act of God is prompted by your faith. Believe that God is all-powerful and can change your situation. Pray for freedom. Bind the spirits that seek to enslave you in a prison of sin. God will free you from your captive as you act on his Word in faith and obedience. He will loose the chains of sickness, poverty, and pain from your life. All you have to do is ask, believe, and receive.

POSSESSING THE PROMISE

*29 **Immediately** her bleeding stopped and she felt in her body that **she was freed** from her suffering.*

John 10:10 says that the thief comes only to steal and kill and destroy but Jesus comes so that you might have life and have it to the full. This full life does not allow for any manner of sickness. It is not God's will for your life. Recognize sickness as an attack from the enemy. God's word tells us that "all" who touched him were healed. It does not say "might be", "could", "can". It says, "were" healed. Draw near to him. In return, he will draw near to you. Within this union, there is not sickness; there is no lack and every manner of sickness within your life will be healed.

The Lord will reward everyone for whatever good he does, whether slave or free. (Ephesians 6:8) "Blessed" knew this. Despite being enslaved by her issue of blood, she recognized that Jesus had a reward for her obedience. She knew that her preparation to receive her blessing would be acknowledged and her diligence honored. Seeking the precepts of God allowed grace to return Blessed to righteousness.

Receiving her freedom demanded that she walk in the righteousness that was hers through Jesus Christ.

Overcoming adversity requires that you do not believe the lies of the enemy. Through Jesus, you are purified from everything that contaminates your body, mind, and spirit and every kind of sickness. God will hold you up with his right hand until you can stand on your own two feet. You will find refuge, protection, and defense in him. He will rescue you from your adversaries. He secures your justice from those who seek to destroy you, even Satan. You are perfected through Jesus Christ. In him, there is a peace that surpasses all understanding. This peace comes from knowing that every one of God's promises will be fulfilled. You are worthy of his blessings and all things will work for your ultimate good. Victory over adversity requires that you take a strategic approach to reclaiming your health, wealth, and your life. Identify the enemy attempting to destroy you. He is a liar and murder. Do not believe anything he tells you. Acknowledge your powerlessness against him without Jesus. Fix your mind on the things of God and walk in obedience and faith. Do not accept anything less for your life than what God's word promises. In doing so, you will realize that any manner of sickness is not an option. Claiming victory requires that you walk in the glory of God, knowing that you are entitled to it. It is yours because Jesus paid the price. Even when the world tells you that you are not worthy, remember that God sees you differently from the way the world looks at you. When he looks at you he sees his beloved son, Jesus who is holy, blameless, and righteous. Overcoming adversity demands that you look at yourself though the same eyes. You are righteousness because Jesus who lives in you is righteous. This righteousness comes by faith. It is an irrevocable gift that comes when you accept Jesus as your savior. It entitles you to all of the privileges of the

King. Kings don't live in poverty, sickness, depression, failure, or any other negative state. Kings reign as an example for others to follow.

Possessing the promise is not just about a tangible blessing. There is a spiritual transference of power through intimacy with him. This power sustains you through whatever life brings. Accept the inheritance laid up in the kingdom for you. In his place of promise, there is comfort for your pain and power over your fears. Bitterness is exchanged with compassion. There is wholeness in your brokenness. There is peace in the mist of turmoil. Here the unclean are made clean. This promise frees the captives from bondage, your faith is redeemed, and you begin to walk in the authority claimed for you on Calvary. In this place of promise Blessed found not only healing but her destiny and so can you.

There is strength and courage in Jesus Christ. Be steadfast. God is with you and if he is with you, who can be against you. Recognize the power of God to provide everything you need and then act on it. Recognize your need for redemption and accept God's Word as your template for life. Trust God. His word promises that his blessings will take sickness from you. This refers to any kind of sickness; mental, physical, emotional, or spiritual. You can live righteous and be made whole. God's word says that you are a joint heir to the kingdom. Claim your inheritance. If it is for your healing, receive it. If it is strength you desire, believe for it. If you seek knowledge and wisdom, claim it. Every one of God's promises can become a reality for your life. The Word says that "all" who touched him were healed. This remains true today. There is power in the hem of his garment.

Receiving healing and restoration requires that you keep your eye on the promise. Walk in obedience and act in faith. Blessed should have been broken, in her body, her spirit, and her mind but she wasn't. She was empowered through God's power to stand in the face of adversity, fully assured of God's plan for her. Blessed was not permitted in crowds because anyone who touched her became unclean. Yet, she was not deterred by what she saw in the natural. She was not intimidated by the large, aggressive, and potentially dangerous crowd. She was in that crowd waiting to receive her healing. She courageously reached out for Jesus even at the cost of physical harm and/or death and he rewarded her diligence. God will reward you over and above all that you can ask and think. He not only rewarded Blessed with healing and restoration, he gave her the gift of life.

HIS POWER

*30 At once **Jesus realized that power had gone out from him**. He turned around in the crowd and asked, **"Who touched my clothes?"***
*31 "You see the people crowding against you," his disciples answered, "and yet you can ask, **'Who touched me?'** "*

Many people in the Bible used a point of contact to grab God's glory. David used his sling slot to release the faith to slay Goliath. Moses used his rod to summon the power of God to roll back the Red Sea. Elijah used his mantle to possess God's power in parting the waters. The Roman centurion used God's Word to heal his servant. Jairus used Jesus' hands to raise his daughter from the dead. None of these points of contact would have been more than mere objects without an intimate relationship with God, fueled by faith and obedience.

Jesus asked, "Who touched my clothes?" for two reasons. The first was because he was seeking praise. Let the righteous rejoice in the LORD and take refuge in him; let all the upright in heart praise him! (Psalms 64:10) Praise is awesome weapon for possessing the promise. Praise God for your victory in faith. Your faith releases blessings over your life. Praise Him for his faithfulness to show up in your times of need. In your weakness, God will make you as bold as a lion. He will help you to speak with assurance even in the face of giants. God desires your praise. It is so important that God appointed an entire group of people, the Levites, to accomplish this task. Praise summons the blessings of God. It allowed the leprotic who returned in thanksgiving to be made completely whole. Praise allowed Jehoshophat to gain victory over his enemies and brought down the walls of Jericho. Praise brings freedom from bondage, sickness, and death. It shields you under the blood of Jesus. As you give praise to God, you may be afflicted but you will not be affected. Praise allows God to bless you in all you do. He will bless you so that others will see his glory and be saved through your testimony.

Jabez, like "Blessed" recognized the importance of praise in claiming and retaining healing and restoration. He knew that with the hand of Jesus upon his life, that he would be kept from harm and free of pain. This hand still provides healing and protection today. It will lift you above your circumstances and to hold you up in times of need. Praise summons God's helping hand to carry you through.

The second reason for asking who touched him was because he desired Blessed's sincere and honest confession. He desires a confession of his Truths over your life and a confession of your sin so that you can be forgiven. Your confessions allow God to gain access into your life so that he can move on your behalf. He desires a pure, sincere, and honest heart willing to offer radical praise through confession of his Truth. Jesus did not ask who touched him because he didn't know. He asked because he was seeking an honest confession as a sign of repentance. James 5:16 says that if you confess your sins and pray for each other, you will be healed. His word commands that every knee will bow and every tongue will confess. Confession allows the Lord will purify you from all unrighteousness. God does not need your confession because he knows every step of your life. Your Confession allows the Lord to relieve you of your guilt. It allows him to forgive you. It as a sign of your willingness to allow him power over your life. Confession frees you from the bondage of sin and brings a renewal of the mind and spirit. Confession brings obedience by removing the distraction and deception that hinders your progress. Confess with your mouth, "Jesus is Lord," and believe in your heart that God raised him from the dead, you will be saved. Proverbs 28:13 says that if you conceal your sins you will not prosper, but if you confesses and renounce them you will find mercy. Confession glorifies God. Confession removes the guilt that hinders the fullness of God.

The word of God says that you will have what you say. Confess the word of God. It is one of you greatest weapons against the attack of the enemy. Whenever Jesus was confronted by the devil he fought back with God's word. In times of attack you must do the same. God's word will give you the courage to overcome any adversary. Rely on the Lord and the power in his Word to give you the strength to endure. Read it, quote it, and sow it in your heart. Confession makes God's power real to you and reveals it to others who might not know him. It says, "My God can do that!" Speak positive confessions over your life knowing that God has the power to make every one of his promises come true. Below I have listed some positive affirmations for you. They have brought me through many trials and as I walk as a restored and whole woman of God, they are still very much a part of my daily existence.

Positive confessions allow you to put your trust in God and to counter the lies of the enemy with Truth; God's truth. Confess the promises of his word. Apply them to your life and your circumstances. Then rest in the refuge of Jesus, knowing that he will do what his word says he will do.

PERCEIVED NEEDS

32 But Jesus kept looking around to see who had done it.

Jesus was looking around to see who had touched him because he perceived the needs of his child. He recognized her need for deliverance and forgiveness. He wanted to bless her openly for her unwavering faith. He recognized her obedience and repentant heart and wanted to honor her with the desires of her heart. Jesus wanted to reveal God's glory so that others would know his power and desire to know him.

Sickness comes in all forms. It can physical where it affects the body or mental where it the mind might be affected. There can be spiritual sickness such as demonic possession or simply, sin. Sickness can emotional as seen in depression, insecurity, and timidity. In other words, anything that goes against the wholeness and joy that the word of God promises is a sickness. It is a tactic of the enemy, Satan, who comes to kill, steal, and destroy. It is sin and must be rebuked.

Rebuking sickness and sin demands that you recognize that Jesus has authority over sickness and death. He allowed power to leave his body to heal Blessed's sickness and to meet her need. But don't think that this power left him without his knowledge or control. His word says that everything is in his control. He allowed Blessed to receive the portion of the grace and mercy needed for her healing. Just like Blessed, he knows what you are going through. A God who knows the number of hairs on your head knows what you have need of and he is willing and prepared to meet every need you have even deliverance from bondage, sickness, and sin.

Mark 1:15 says, "The time has come", he said. "The kingdom of God is near. Repent and believe the good news!" Blessed did just that. At the time she reached out to Jesus, all she had left was faith. After hearing the good news about Jesus, she realized that twelve years of suffering, disappointment, and isolation was long enough. Her total dependence was on Jesus. It was God's time for her to reach out in faith and claim what God had for her. She recognized the importance of getting in the presence of God. As she bowed down at Jesus' feet, she repented in obedience. She believed the good news so much so that she was in the right place at the right time to claim all that God had for her; healing, redemption, and restoration.

Deliverance from sin requires repentance. Repentance recognizes your need for redemption. Repentance allows God to forgive you. It tells him that you have made a conscious choice to put him first and that his plans for your life are important. It shows him that you are in agreement with the path for your life that he has laid before you. It requires that you become totally dependent on Jesus and affirms your powerlessness without Jesus and your strength in him. Accept the gospel as "good news". Allow God to order your steps by operating in love, patience, and humility.

Repentance acknowledges that you forgive yourself, God, and anyone who has wronged you. Forgiveness allows you to claim what belongs to you. Forgiveness allows to you be completely healed. There is no sin too great to be forgiven. (Colossians 3:13) says that you must forgive as God has forgiven you. Recognize the shame, bitterness, and disappointment that Satan has placed on your heart as sin. Confess it and believe for the memory of whatever you have done wrongly to be removed. Once this is done, accept your forgiveness, it is done. God's word says so. Once you are forgiven, profess your forgiveness and do not allow Satan to tell you otherwise. "Jesus forgives all sins and heals all your diseases." (Psalms 103:3) As Satan tries to bring the thoughts of your past to you, rebuke him immediately. Do not allow his lies to distort your truth for one minute.

Forgiveness is usually a three fold process. God's word requires that you forgive anyone whom you think might have harmed you, including God and yourself. Your first step is to forgive yourself. It allows you to see yourself worthy of the calling and blessings of God. If Blessed had not forgiven herself would she have been equipped to reach out for her healing? Certainly not. She would have cowered away under the lie that she was not worthy of his God's blessings. She would have believed that she did not deserve the right to touch Jesus or to claim her inheritance. As you forgive yourself, you are able to see the love of God and his mercy. You recognize his compassion to forgive every offense. You will understand the sin of aut against God because his word says that you must reconcile your unforgiveness before offering yourself to God. (Matthew 5:23-24) He will not bring pain and difficulty in your life. These things are of the Devil. As you recognize this tactic of

the devil and rebuke it the sin bitterness and unforgiveness towards others will be revealed to you. Satan's evil
schemes will become real to you and through this clarity
you will understand the importance of total forgiveness
to total repentance and restoration. One can't happen
without the other.

God's forgiveness requires that you confess your sin
and repent. Jesus did not ask who touched him because
he did not know. He is omnipotent, nothing happens
without his knowledge. Whatever you have done is a
minor infraction when placed against the forgiveness of
God. Once you repent, Jesus will remember your sins
no more. Remember this promise when the enemy
comes to condemn you. He will tell you that your sins
are to great to be forgiven or your sickness is too severe
to be healed. It is a lie from the pit of Hell. The blood
of Jesus was poured out for your sins. Claim your healing and restoration and believe that it is yours. Your
debt was paid on Calvary. Forgive yourself and allow
God to forgive you. Mark 11:25 says that "if you hold
anything against anyone, **including yourself**, forgive
him so that God can forgive you." {emphasis mine}

If you ever question your ability to claim or retain
your healing, simply look at the example set by Jesus.
He went throughout all the land healing "every sickness" that was brought before him. An when the enemy
came to challenge his purpose, his work, his place in the
kingdom he replied, "Go tell that fox, 'I will drive out
demons and heal people today and tomorrow, and on the
third day I will reach my goal.' You are that person
whom he is healing today and tomorrow until he
reaches his goal. Healing and restoration are yours because he said it is. You like Jesus must not be deterred
as you face the trials of life. Keep pressing on toward
your purpose and God's plan for your life. Stand on his
promises fully assured that, through God, all things are
possible and all things will work for your ultimate good.

OUT OF THE HEART THE MOUTH SPEAKS

33 *Then the woman, knowing what had happened to her, came and* **fell at his feet** *and, trembling with fear,* **told him the whole truth.**

God is all knowing and all-powerful. He did not ask who touched him because he needed to know. He already knew. He asked because he was seeking a humble and honest confession. Blessed was humbled through her repeated failure and disappointment. Her sickness and numerous failed attempts to acquire healing left her desperate with nowhere else to turn. Out of desperation, she submitted in humility. Humility allowed God to work on her behalf. It allowed her to reach out to the only person who could heal her, Jesus. Blessed like the Israelites was lead through a desert. God did this so that he might reveal what was in their heart. He was seeking for his glory to be revealed and sincere praise for his works. God desires your praise not out of pride or arrogance but because he desires for others to come to know him.

"The humble are greatest in his kingdom." (Matthew 18:4) Humility shelters you from the trials of life by allowing the

Lord to cover you. He will hide the humble from destruction and deliver them from whatever seeks to destroy them. Humility allows the Lord to hear you and you to hear him. It fosters faith, frees your will, and brings wisdom. This wisdom helps you to recognize God's greatness and faithfulness to meet your needs. Humility brings favor. Favor will allow you to healed from the same ailments and illness that others around you are dying from. Terminal illnesses will be cured. Bitterness will be removed. Love will abound and abundant life will be yours; not by your will, but by his. The battle is not yours but the Lord's. Pray and seek his face in the midst of your trials. He will hear you. He will forgive your sins and heal you. Humility allows God to respond to your prayers and to evoke a reverent fear of God that allows him to order your steps in your predestined direction. It rebukes pride and brings life. It allows God the freedom to propel you into the place of righteousness that was reserved for you at the cross and provides freedom from bondage, guidance, and prosperity today, tomorrow, and forever.

Do not overlook the "due time" aspect of humility. 1 Peter 5:6 says "humble yourselves, therefore, under God's mighty hand, that he may lift you up in due time" Everything that happens in your life will be in God's time not yours. God does not operate within out time restraints. Many people attempt to bargain with God. Some say, "Okay Lord, if you do _____ for me, I will do _____ for you." God can not be bartered with or bought. He knows the path of your life. This path may get cluttered by the trials and tribulation of life but at the end is the life of abundance that God's word promises. This race can only be finished through faith and perseverance. Humility allows God to go with you up this path, to stand beside you in battle, and to carry you through when you get weary.

The Lord might lead you into a desert, as well. Relying on Jesus will help you to take the shortcut through the deserts of life and removes the disappointment and desperation you experience as you take the long way around because of your disobedience. Your trials like Blessed and the Israelites will humble you and test you so that God will know what is in your heart. Will you keep his commands as you face adversity, sickness, or death or will you give up? Will you stand on his promises knowing that his word is true? Success in the face of adversity requires that you remember that he will never leave you nor forsake you. You are powerlessness to control your circumstances without him. Draw near to God and see if he doesn't elevate you above your circumstances. He will purify your heart, mind, body, and soul. He will supply you with fresh manna in your hunger, clothing in your nakedness, and protection, strength, and healing according to your needs. When you feel you have no where else to turn focus your attention on the heavenly Father. Submit to him in humility and allow him to exalt you to a place where your life glorifies him. In this place, there is no sickness, no lack, no loss.

MUSTARD SEEDS, MULBERRY TREES, & MOUNTAINS

34 *He said to her,* ***"Daughter, your faith has healed you.*** *Go in* ***peace*** *and* ***be freed*** *from your suffering."*

Many others in the bible used faith to receive healing and restoration. Faith allowed crippled men to walk, the blind to see, and the dumb to speak. It allowed sickness to be healed and death to be reversed. In Matthew 9, the paralytic was healed by faith. Abraham claimed healing for his wife's barrenness with his faith. The blind men received their sight by faith. In Matthew 15, faith allowed the Canaanite woman to claim healing from demonic possession for her daughter. Faith allowed the Centurion to claim healing for his servant who was facing inevitable death. Faith allowed the ten men with leprosy to be healed and one to be made completely whole. "Blessed" healed by faith and so can you.

Faith is the master key to achieving and maintaining success in every aspect of life. Faith brings the peace of God. It brings the forgiveness of sins and removes condemnation which is of the devil. Faith nurtures obedience, discipline, and growth. Faith allowed Jesus to fulfill the plan and purpose for his life without resistance or hesitance. It will do the same in your life. It will take your mind off of your situations and focus your heart and mind on the things of God. Faith will help you to see past your hurts to your healing, your brokenness to your restoration, your bitterness to love and life. It justifies you as a joint heir to the kingdom of God and all of its riches.

Without faith, it is impossible to please God. Satan will use your distrusts and disappointments to steal whatever God has for you. Faith removes Satan's power over you and acknowledges God as your deliverer and freedom as your destiny. John 14:22 says that anyone who has faith will perform even greater works than Jesus. This scripture provides undeniable evidence that healing others and healing yourself is a reality through faith. No matter what you are battling in life, faith in Jesus can help you to overcome it. No matter how immense or perilous your adversary is, God will equip you for the battle. All things are possible with God.

"Blessed's" faith allowed her to accept that Jesus was coming and that he could heal her. When she reached out to touch the hem of Jesus' garment, she did so in faith. She formed the thought in her mind and then acted on it, solely based on what she had heard about Jesus. But her statement, "I will be healed" says that she trusted that he would heal her. Even without a full understanding of his power and grace, Blessed knew that she would bed healed. But without faith, it is impossible to please God. Without faith her "will" would have become a might or a maybe and she would have missed her blessing. The strength Blessed found in Jesus allowed her to reach out and touch the untouchable. The accompanying wisdom helped her to see necessity of her actions to fulfill her destiny. Faith allowed her to be healed instantly and completely restored.

Luke 17:6 says that if you have faith as small as a mustard seed, you can say to the mulberry tree, 'Be up-rooted and planted in the sea,' and it will obey you. John 8:32 says if the son, Jesus Christ, sets you free, you will be free indeed. To overcome the trials of life, you must learn to walk in obedience, faith, perseverance, strength and be willing to fight for what you know God has promised you. Do not get weary in fulfilling your purpose because all things will work for your ultimate good. 1 Corinthians 5:4 tells us that when we assemble in the name of our Lord Jesus that he and his power are with us. This is the same power that allowed many to be healed in biblical times. It is the same power by which many are still being healed today. This power healed Blessed from her infirmity and me from the trauma of my abuse. It is by this power your healing will come, as well.

Blessed's healing was not a temporary healing but a permanent deliverance from bondage. It was a spiritual evolution. The halt of her bleeding not only ended her suffering and but freed her to worship God in body, spirit, and truth. It freed her to walk in love again and to share the love of God with others through her confession. It restored her life. My healing was much like hers. As I was delivered from an abusive spouse I evolved as well. I was transformed from a bitter and broken believer to an empowered woman of God, fully assured in my purpose and God's plan for my life. I am fulfilling that purpose by sharing my story every chance I get. In my transformation, I learned that the heavenly Father desires for me to be whole. He desires for me to walk tall and stand strong so that others can see him in me.

Still not convinced of God's power and his love? Think of Paul during the sail to Crete. (see Acts 27) He knew that because the angel of the Lord was with him, "not one would be lost". The angel of the Lord is with you also. Jesus healed Blessed from her infirmity, he healed me from my abuse, and he will heal you. His word promises that not one of you will be lost. Everything will happen just as his word promises. Healing and restoration are yours because his word promises it. He will strengthen your mind so that you will recognize the vision he sees in you. He will strengthen your body so that you have the power through him to fight for what is yours.

Do not let life and its circumstances limit you. The enemy will try to place limits on your mind, body, finances; and your soul. But remember that Satan is a defeated foe.

Jesus purchased your victory on Calvary with his blood. No matter what life puts before you, do not let it stop you from claiming your blessings. God has a plan for your life. Everything you do is in preparation for fulfilling that purpose. Make a choice to answer the call by receiving the daily lessons set before you with humility and faith. God honors faith no matter how small. His word says that if you have faith of a "grain of a mustard seed" that we can move mountains. You can heal sickness and disease and claim fulfill your destiny. But only if you believe and receive the Word of God . Trust God and victory in every area of your life is yours. If you serve the limitless God I serve, there are no limits to where life can take you. You can win over adversity.

Most importantly, remember that everything you need lies in Jesus Christ. He is the answer. In times of illness, depression, and disappointment, the word of God serves as a tool of eternal solace and strength. Power lies in your commitment and obedience to God and his mandates for your life. This power fuels a desire to live out the perfect will of God. He promises you health, prosperity, joy, love, and peace. The woman with the issue of blood, through her trial, has shown you how to claim your inheritance. Now it is your turn. Press toward the high calling of God. Press past your limitations and shortcomings. Do not be deterred. Everything that God says is yours is waiting for you. As you achieve victory and success in life you will find that fulfilling your destiny is more than surviving it is thriving. Like the woman with the issue of blood and me, you have been predestined to do so.

Living a life that is pleasing and claiming all that he has for you requires four simple steps. The woman with the issue of blood used these very steps to gain her healing and to fulfill her destiny. That destiny was to show us how to fulfill God's plan for our lives. First speak success and blessings into existence. Blessed did this when she said, "If I touch the hem of his garment, I **will** be healed". Then we must act in faith. She touched the hem of Jesus' garment. Without acting on her confession her words would have fallen void to the ground. Receive the blessings of God, recognizing him as your source. Blessed received her healing and confessed Jesus as her healer. Lastly, we must share our testimony to glorify God so that others will desire to know him. The word says that Blessed told the "whole truth". As she did this the word says that she was freed from her suffering. As we confess him as our savior, we too will find freedom. Fear, sickness, and sin runs in the presence of a bold testimony in faith. Use her example and be "Blessed".

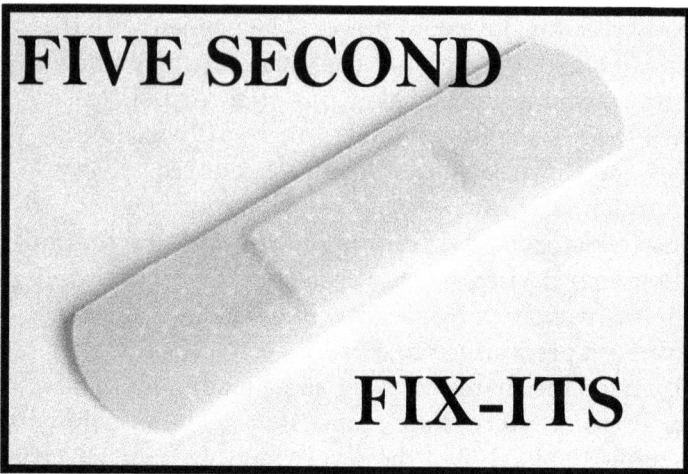

FIVE SECOND FIX-ITS

Designed for Destiny!

ANGER

"I will not be angry or stir up dissension. I recognize this as sin. I don't have a right to be angry with anyone when God has had so much compassion on me."

NOTES

_____

_____

_____

_____

_____

_____

_____

_____

_____

_____

_____

_____

_____

_____

_____

BITTERNESS

I recognize that bitterness grieves the Holy Spirit of God. So, today I rid myself of all bitterness. I will be kind, compassionate, and forgiving to others, just as in Christ God forgave you.

NOTES

_____

_____

_____

_____

_____

_____

_____

_____

_____

_____

_____

_____

_____

CONTROLLING YOUR TONGUE

"The Spirit of the LORD spoke through me;
his word was on my tongue. My tongue will
speak of your righteousness and of your
praises all day long."

NOTES

_____

_____

_____

_____

_____

_____

_____

_____

_____

_____

_____

_____

_____

DESPERATION

"In my desperation, I recognize your ability to rescue me from those who pursue me, to deliver me from the curses of my fathers, and to meet me right where I am with grace and mercy."

NOTES

_____

_____

_____

_____

_____

_____

_____

_____

_____

_____

_____

_____

_____

DIRECTION

"I know that my steps are ordered by you. I will follow the path that you have set before me knowing that joy and eternal pleasures lie along this path."

NOTES

_____

_____

_____

_____

_____

_____

_____

_____

_____

_____

_____

_____

_____

_____

_____

_____

DISAPPOINTMENT

"I will trust in you. I know that you hear my cries and that you are faithful to do what you word says you will do."

NOTES

_____

_____

_____

_____

_____

_____

_____

_____

_____

_____

_____

_____

_____

_____

_____

DOUBT

"I am stable in all my ways. I am sure of God's love for me and his faithfulness fulfill all of his promises. Abundance is mine because God's word says it is."

NOTES

_____

_____

_____

_____

_____

_____

_____

_____

_____

_____

_____

_____

_____

_____

_____

_____

FAITH

"I believe that you are not a man who would lie. I believe that what your word says is true will come to past and all things will work for my ultimate good."

NOTES

_____

_____

_____

_____

_____

_____

_____

_____

_____

_____

_____

_____

_____

_____

_____

_____

_____

FEAR

"I am protected from the lash of the tongue,
and need not fear when destruction comes.
In righteousness I am be established. I have
nothing to fear."

NOTES

_____

_____

_____

_____

_____

_____

_____

_____

_____

_____

_____

_____

_____

_____

_____

FREEDOM

"The Lord is the Spirit, and where the Spirit of the Lord is, there is freedom. I will walk about in freedom, for I have sought out His precepts."

NOTES

_____

_____

_____

_____

_____

_____

_____

_____

_____

_____

_____

_____

_____

_____

_____

_____

FRUSTRATION

"I recognize that frustration is the work of the evildoer. I refuse to live in sin but will allow the fruits of the spirit, love, joy, peace, patience, kindness, goodness, faithfulness, gentleness and self-control to operate in my life because I know that these confuse the enemy and please the Lord."

NOTES

_____

_____

_____

_____

_____

_____

_____

_____

_____

_____

GUILT

"My heart is cleanse from a guilty conscience and my body is washed with pure
water. I know that you are the only true
judge and in your compassion and grace I
am forgiven."

NOTES

_____

_____

_____

_____

_____

_____

_____

_____

_____

_____

_____

_____

_____

_____

HEALING

"Your light will break forth like the dawn,
and your healing will quickly appear; the
glory of the LORD is my rear guard. By
your stripes I am healed. "

NOTES

_____

_____

_____

_____

_____

_____

_____

_____

_____

_____

_____

_____

_____

_____

_____

_____

INSECURITY

"All things are possible with my God. I am not what the enemy says I am but what you say I am. I am righteous, whole, and blameless and more than a conqueror through Christ Jesus."

NOTES

_____

_____

_____

_____

_____

_____

_____

_____

_____

_____

_____

_____

_____

_____

JEALOUSY

"I will not covet the blessings of my brothers and sisters. I recognize jealousy as an obvious act of sin. I want to inherit the kingdom therefore I will walk in thanksgiving and give praise in all things."

NOTES

_____

_____

_____

_____

_____

_____

_____

_____

_____

_____

_____

_____

_____

JUSTICE

"Justice is mine through my righteousness in Christ Jesus. He will
avenge."

NOTES

_____
_____
_____
_____
_____
_____
_____
_____
_____
_____
_____
_____
_____
_____
_____
_____

LAZINESS

"Lazy hands make a man poor, but diligent hands bring wealth. I, through faith and patience, will inherit what has been promised."

NOTES

_____

_____

_____

_____

_____

_____

_____

_____

_____

_____

_____

_____

_____

_____

_____

_____

LONELINESS

"I am not alone because you are always with me. You will never leave me nor forsake me."

NOTES

_____
_____
_____
_____
_____
_____
_____
_____
_____
_____
_____
_____
_____
_____
_____
_____
_____

LUST

"I put to death things of my earthly nature including lust. I recognize this idolatry as sin and I will have no other God before you."

NOTES

_____

_____

_____

_____

_____

_____

_____

_____

_____

_____

_____

_____

_____

_____

_____

_____

PATIENCE

"I will be still and wait on the Lord for he knows the path that I should take."

NOTES

_____
_____
_____
_____
_____
_____
_____
_____
_____
_____
_____
_____
_____
_____
_____
_____
_____

PEACE

"My covenant of peace is with the Lord therefore I will not be dismayed. I have a peace that surpasses all understanding."

NOTES

_____

_____

_____

_____

_____

_____

_____

_____

_____

_____

_____

_____

_____

_____

_____

_____

_____

PHYSICAL PAIN

"I am free of pain because you hand is upon me and your salvation will free me from the bondage of my illness and the grasp of the enemy."

NOTES

_____

_____

_____

_____

_____

_____

_____

_____

_____

_____

_____

_____

_____

_____

_____

_____

_____

PRIDE

"To fear the LORD is to hate evil; I hate pride and arrogance, evil behavior and perverse speech. I have great confidence in you and I take great pride in you. In you I am greatly encouraged."

NOTES

_____

_____

_____

_____

_____

_____

_____

_____

_____

_____

_____

_____

_____

_____

_____

_____

PROTECTION

"Though they plot against me and devise wicked schemes, they cannot succeed. The Lord is my rock, my fortress, and my deliverer. He is my shield and the horn of my salvation. The Lord provides refuge from my oppression. He is my stronghold in times of trouble."

NOTES

_____

_____

_____

_____

_____

_____

_____

_____

_____

_____

_____

_____

SADNESS

"I will rejoice even in my affliction because I know you know the anguish in my soul and are faithful to heal me. My God will heal my broken heart and bind up my wounds so that I will be whole again."

NOTES

_____
_____
_____
_____
_____
_____
_____
_____
_____
_____
_____
_____
_____
_____

SHYNESS/TIMIDNESS

"I am righteous through Christ Jesus and as bold as a lion. I am not what the world but what God says I am. I am blameless and righteous through Christ Jesus."

NOTES

_____

_____

_____

_____

_____

_____

_____

_____

_____

_____

_____

_____

_____

_____

SIN/DISOBEDIENCE

"I will let no wrongdoing be found in me as long as I live. I will not sin with my words, thoughts, or deeds. I am righteous because I sit at your feet and righteousness and justice are the foundation of your throne."

NOTES

_____

_____

_____

_____

_____

_____

_____

_____

_____

_____

_____

_____

_____

_____

SORROW/MOURNING

"Today I bathe myself in the oil of gladness knowing that it washes away all sorrow and pain."

NOTES

_____
_____
_____
_____
_____
_____
_____
_____
_____
_____
_____
_____
_____
_____
_____

STRENGTH

"I can do all things through Christ Jesus"
who strengthens me. I am empowered for
whatever life brings before me, because Jesus lives in me"

NOTES

_____

_____

_____

_____

_____

_____

_____

_____

_____

_____

_____

_____

_____

_____

SUCCESS

"I will commit to the Lord in everything I do because I know that God will give me the desires of my heart and make all of my plans succeed."

NOTES

_____

_____

_____

_____

_____

_____

_____

_____

_____

_____

_____

_____

_____

_____

UNLOVED

"I am loved because I am just and your un-
failing love never forsakes your faithful
ones."

NOTES

_____

_____

_____

_____

_____

_____

_____

_____

_____

_____

_____

_____

_____

_____

_____

_____

VICTORY

"The LORD is with me to fight for me against my enemies to give me **victory**. I am victorious because the battle has already been won."

NOTES

_____

_____

_____

_____

_____

_____

_____

_____

_____

_____

_____

_____

_____

_____

_____

WISDOM

"My mouth will speak words of wisdom as the utterance from your heart gives me understanding."

NOTES

_____

_____

_____

_____

_____

_____

_____

_____

_____

_____

_____

_____

_____

_____

WORRY

I will not worry about life. I will not worry about tomorrow, for tomorrow will worry about itself. I know that you will give me words and wisdom that none of my adversaries will be able to resist or contradict."

NOTES

_____
_____
_____
_____
_____
_____
_____
_____
_____
_____
_____
_____
_____
_____